Surviving the Earthquake

Written by Nancy O'Connor

Illustrated by Meredith Thomas

Flying Start
to Literacy®

Contents

Chapter 1

Sammy's story

Sammy drove the football hard downfield, dodging his opponents. The moment he saw an opening, he kicked. The ball shot right past the goalie. Goal! Sammy fist-pumped high in the air. His team had won! All his teammates ran over and slapped him on the back.

"Nice job, Sammy," called Pierre, who was on the other team. "But we'll get even with you tomorrow."

Sammy wiped the sweat from his forehead and looked down the hill, towards the ocean and the city of Port-au-Prince. Even with the sea breeze, his damp T-shirt clung to his chest, and he was parched.

He tucked the ball under his arm and waved goodbye to his teammates, Marcel and Jose. As he turned towards home, Manno bounded up to him, barking and wagging his tail. Sammy knelt and gave the big dog a hug. He remembered when the dog had first come to live with his family as a skinny, frightened puppy. That had been nearly five years ago – right after the terrible earthquake.

*****

Back then, Sammy was in the first grade. It had been an ordinary school day. At the end of the day, Sammy and Marcel ran out to the field behind the school and sat on the grass to watch the older boys play football. Sammy loved football more than anything. Recently, his father had taken him to see the national team play. Sammy wanted to be a famous football player, just like his hero, Manno Sanon, the greatest Haitian player of all time.

As Sammy leant back on his elbows to watch the game, he felt something warm and furry brush past his arm.

"It's that pup again," said Sammy, as he patted the small brown puppy. "That dog follows me everywhere."

"I wonder why," said Marcel, cheekily.

"No idea," said Sammy as he opened his lunch box and scooped up the remains of his favourite snack – fried yams. When he held out his hand, the puppy crept closer.

"Go ahead," Sammy said. "It's okay."

The dog gobbled the yams and looked up with dark, hungry eyes. Sammy patted him gently on the head, then scratched behind his ears. "I wish I could have a dog, but Mama doesn't want an animal around my baby sister. She says dogs are dirty and have fleas."

"What does your papa say?" Marcel asked.

Sammy laughed. "He always says, 'Ask your mama.'"

Suddenly the puppy began to quiver and whimper as if he was terrified of something.

"Listen," Marcel said, holding up one hand. "Can you hear other dogs barking?" From around the city, it seemed there was a chorus of barking and howling.

"Calm down, pup," said Sammy.

"I don't like it," said Marcel. "Maybe we should go home."

Sammy and Marcel headed for home, with the puppy closer than ever behind them. Sammy remembered the coins in his pocket and told Marcel he wanted to stop at the little grocery shop near his apartment to buy a cold drink.

"Okay, I'll see you tomorrow." Marcel waved as he walked away.

Sammy entered the shop, shutting the door behind him. The puppy stared at him through the glass and scratched at the door.

"Make your dog stop that," said the shopkeeper.

"He's not my dog," Sammy explained. "He just follows me. I don't know what's wrong with him."

Sammy walked through the crowded aisles towards the refrigerator case in the back corner where the soft drinks were kept. Just as he opened the glass door of the case and reached for a cold drink, he heard a loud, rumbling sound, as if a huge truck was roaring right through the shop.

The floor started to tremble beneath his feet, and the
building seemed to tilt as cans of food toppled off the
shelves around him. The thundering noise grew louder,
and the floor moved up and down, like ocean waves.
Sammy lurched from side to side and quickly crouched
low near a wooden counter. Pieces of ceiling plaster
rained down around him. He heard the shopkeeper
scream, "Earthquake!" as he ran from the shop.

Boom! The glass windows at the front of the shop exploded.
The refrigerator case fell forwards and crashed. Stacks of
groceries spilled over, burying Sammy beneath them. A
metal shelf slammed down on his arm, and Sammy heard
the bone snap. He screamed, just as the ceiling collapsed.

Chapter 2

Daniel's story

Daniel tucked his yellow fire helmet under his arm and scooped up his duffle bag. It had been one day since the earthquake had struck Haiti and Daniel's plane had just touched down at the Port-au-Prince airport. Daniel followed the other firefighters out of the plane. Standing at the top of the stairs, he looked around and gasped. It was early evening. The hillsides were covered with the rubble of ruined houses. The airport runway had gaping holes in it. Even the control tower was damaged. Yesterday's 7.0 earthquake had caused all this devastation in Port-au-Prince and across the island country of Haiti.

As darkness descended over the city, Daniel could see bright islands of light. Although the city had lost all power, there were two playing fields with solar-powered street lights. People were flocking there to set up camps.

Daniel had only been with the Miami Fire Department for a month. This was his first disaster assignment. He was here with his fellow firefighters to help search for and rescue people affected by the quake. Even though he'd only just graduated from the Fire Academy, Daniel had been asked to volunteer because he spoke Haitian-Creole, the language of Haiti. His parents had moved from Port-au-Prince to Florida when he was just a baby. He was proud to be here, but a little scared, too. He saw now what a huge job lay ahead of him and his fellow firefighters.

"Let's get the trucks loaded," the captain called to the men. Daniel helped put the tools and first aid supplies they had brought into the back of the truck. Then he and his buddies climbed in, and they drove off towards the city.

It was a slow trip. Streets were blocked with piles of concrete, smashed cars and toppled telephone poles. Hundreds of crying and injured people wandered in the wreckage. Everywhere Daniel looked there were scenes of destruction.

With no time to waste, Daniel and his team were assigned to an area. Although it was now nighttime, Daniel and his team had solar-powered torches and lanterns with them so they were able to work into the night.

The team gathered near a huge mound of rubble that had been an apartment building.

"Let's get to work," said the captain. "People are trapped under those concrete beams."

Daniel put on his helmet, a mask and heavy gloves. The crew unloaded shovels, jackhammers and concrete saws. One man set up the fibre optic camera he would use to locate victims under the rubble.

The firefighters worked for hours, taking breaks only to grab sandwiches and water. The crew had hung the solar lanterns from cables stretched across the streets. Every time a person was rescued, cheers went up from the crew and the people gathered nearby.

By early morning, just as he was about to climb into the truck to go to the tent camp that had been set up for rescue workers, Daniel heard a dog whining. He looked around and saw a scrawny puppy across the street, in front of the ruins of a small shop. He was digging in the rubble.

"Hurry up, Daniel!" called one of the crew members. "Let's go get some sleep. We have to be back here in a couple hours."

"Coming," Daniel replied. "I'm about to fall asleep standing up." He climbed into the truck with a sigh. He ached all over from lifting heavy chunks of concrete all night. The truck drove off, and Daniel forgot about the puppy.

Chapter 3

Sammy's story

Sammy slowly woke up. It was dark, and his right arm felt as if it was on fire. He tried to move, but he was trapped under something very heavy. How much time had passed? Sammy had no idea and he was frightened. "Mama, Papa, where are you?" Hot tears rolled down his cheeks. He realised no one knew where he was.

His head throbbed, and his throat was dry and filled with dust. He felt around with his left hand and touched something cold and sticky. It was a soft drink can that had been punctured. He pulled it to his mouth, tilted it up and sucked some of the sweet cola out of the hole in the can's side. Nothing had ever tasted so good.

People were shouting far away. Sammy thought he heard a dog barking. "Help! I'm here, I'm here!" he yelled, but his cries came out like squawks.

No one came. Finally, he closed his eyes and slept again.
He had dreams about football, and his father, and the
last game they had gone to together.

A stomachache woke Sammy the next time. He didn't
know if it was day or night. How long had he been
trapped? He was hungry. He stretched his arm out and
something crinkled as his fingers touched it. Paper? He
gripped a corner and pulled the object closer. He sniffed.
A chocolate bar!

A loud rattling startled Sammy. Rescuers must be outside. Someone would find him now, he just knew it. Sammy yelled as loudly as he could. "Help me. I'm trapped. Help!"

He heard a dog barking. Was it the puppy? Could he still be waiting outside the shop? Sammy hoped the puppy's cries would bring help. He began singing Haiti's national anthem, just like he and Papa did whenever they went to a football game.

"For our country,
For our forefathers . . ."

Chapter 4

Daniel's story

It was midday when Daniel and the fire crew returned to the area where they had worked the day before. It was Day 3 of the rescue operation, and time was running out for the people who were trapped in the rubble. Serious injuries and lack of food and water meant some people might not survive much longer.

"Hey, take a look at that dog." Daniel pointed to the puppy across the street. "He's still there." He went over to the puppy and offered him some of his lunch. The animal gulped it down then looked at Daniel and barked.

"I'll bet you're thirsty, too," he said.

Daniel poured some water from his canteen into his helmet and put it on the ground. The dog lapped it up greedily.

"Hey, slow down," said Daniel, "water is scarce around here."

Since the earthquake, there was no clean water supply. The water was contaminated and had to be purified. The dog lapped up the last drips of water and barked again.

"I've got to get to work, buddy. We've got people to rescue."

Daniel shook the water out of his helmet, buckled it under his chin and returned to the crew. Just as he picked up his shovel, he felt a tug on his pant leg. It was the dog again.

"Leave us alone, dog," one of the firefighters said. "Shoo! Go beg somewhere else."

"Wait, guys. I think he's trying to tell me something," Daniel said. He turned and pointed across the street. "He's been sitting over there for the past 24 hours, maybe longer. It makes me wonder why. I'm going to take a look."

He followed the dog back to the ruins and stood for a
moment, listening. Did he hear singing? It sounded like
a song he knew – it was the Haitian national anthem.
Daniel remembered it from his childhood. Someone was
buried in that building – and they were singing.

"Hey, guys, we've got a survivor over here!" he yelled.

Chapter 5

Sammy's story

Sammy heard people shouting, followed by the sounds of machinery and shovels striking stone. "We're on our way!" someone yelled. "Keep singing!"

They had heard him! Sammy tried to sing louder. His throat ached and he could barely lift his head, but he sang.

"United let us march,
Let there be no traitors in our ranks!"

Suddenly, torches pierced the darkness around Sammy. Faces appeared overhead shouting in a language Sammy struggled to understand. When someone lifted the steel shelf off of his broken arm, Sammy yelped.

"We need a splint over here," Daniel called out. "It's okay, son. We'll get you out as soon as we stabilise your arm."

Sammy was frightened by all the noise and the blazing lights. He couldn't understand the rescuers. But then Daniel began to sing while he gently wrapped Sammy's arm in an elastic bandage.

"United let us march,
Let there be no traitors in our ranks!"

Sammy tried to smile through his tears as Daniel lifted him out of the ruins and carried him in his arms, singing to him the whole time.

When they reached the street, Sammy blinked in the bright sunshine. People cheered and clapped as he was loaded into an ambulance. Daniel tucked the boy's backpack on the stretcher beside him.

"That little puppy saved your life, young man," Daniel said. "We've seen him outside this shop every day since we got here."

Sammy lifted his head to look around, but the ambulance doors slammed shut and the vehicle started up the street towards the tent hospital at the stadium. Sammy couldn't see the little dog trotting behind it, but Daniel did.

*****

When Sammy woke up the next morning, Mama and Papa stood by his bed. Mama held Layla, and all three of them were crying.

"Oh, Sammy!" his mother cried. "We thought we had lost you forever."

"We searched and searched for you," his father said. "Everywhere – the school, the playing field, everywhere, but you were nowhere to be found."

"It is a miracle the rescuers discovered you still alive after three whole days," Mama said. "A miracle!"

"No, Mama. Not a miracle," Sammy said, smiling through his own tears. "It was a dog."

"A dog?"

"Yes, the stray puppy that follows me to school every day. He tried to warn me of the earthquake with his barking, and he showed the rescue man were I was. If we can find him, do you think I could keep him?"

"Finding him will not be a problem." Papa gave Sammy a big smile. "He refuses to go away. That puppy has been sitting outside this hospital tent waiting for you. The doctors won't let him inside, but, yes, I think that puppy is now yours to keep."

Just then Sammy's eyes grew wide. Someone was singing the national anthem, right outside the tent. A young firefighter stepped through the doorway and cleared his throat. "I don't mean to interrupt," said Daniel in Creole, "but I wanted to see how this fellow was doing. I'm Daniel, the one who found him."

Sammy's mother's face lit up when she heard Daniel's voice.

"You speak Creole? Thank you! Thank you so much for saving our son."

Papa almost shook Daniel's hand off. "Thank you so much for bringing our boy back to us," Papa said.

"It's my job," Daniel said, "but that little puppy out there helped."

Just then, a flash of fur flew up onto the bed and snuggled next to Sammy. Sammy put his good arm around the puppy and the puppy licked his face.

"Meet Manno," said Sammy with a big grin.

Chapter 6

After the earthquake

So much in Haiti had changed since the earthquake.
Sammy looked down at his right arm and rubbed the
long scar. It was where the bone had been broken in the
earthquake. It had healed well, but sometimes it ached.
He tossed the football from hand to hand as he hurried
down the street towards home. Manno was now a big
dog and still followed him everywhere. It was almost
dark, and he noticed the solar street lights coming on.

Sammy knew that his family had been very lucky.
They had lost all their belongings and their apartment
building had been damaged, but at least they had
survived. Hundreds of thousands of people lost their
lives, and many more had been left homeless.

Fortunately, Mama and Layla had been at the park when the earthquake struck, so they were safe. Papa often spoke of the two terrifying days it took to make his way home from the port and find his family – only to discover Sammy was missing. It took two more days before he and Mama had found Sammy – bruised, cut and with a plaster cast on his arm – in the tent hospital at the stadium. Sammy often thought of Daniel, the Haitian-American firefighter who had rescued him.

For weeks after the disaster, Sammy's family lived in a tent on the playing field near the ruins of his old school. Life in the camp was hard. The tents were made from old sheets that they tied to branches cut down from the trees around the park. But when it rained, water dripped inside. Eventually, some people came in a truck and provided some plastic sheeting to put over the top.

Another day, the same people brought torches. They said that the torches only needed the light from the sun to work. Sammy put his torch outside all day and that night he couldn't believe it. He had light at night for the first time. When he turned on his torch, he could see Mama smiling.

But Sammy's strongest memory was when they finally had lots of clean water. At first, the only clean water flowed from a broken pipe that stuck out of the ground. Sammy and his mother went everyday with a bucket and a plastic bottle to fill. Some people just went to a stream that flowed down one side of the park.

"Never drink the water from that stream," said Mama. "It's dirty and will make us all sick."

Then Papa found out about a large water filter that had been found in the rubble. It had a solar-powered pump so it could provide lots of clean water once it was fixed.

Sammy watched as Papa and two of the other men from the camp pulled it out from the rubble. Many other people came to watch, too. The sun went down and it got dark, but they didn't want to stop working. Everyone from the camp got their solar torches and stood around and shone them so they could still see. Late that night, when the torches were beginning to fade, they finished fixing the machine.

Papa was tired but happy. "All it needs is the sun to charge it," he said. "And we have plenty of sunshine in Haiti. Tomorrow there will be clean water for everyone."

As the days passed, Sammy's family got used to life in the camp. After they had been in the camp for eight months, they were able to return to their home. While most people had lost their homes in the earthquake, their apartment building was only damaged. Sammy's family had been lucky.

Now, five years later, Sammy and Layla attend a brand new school where she is in kindergarten and he is in sixth grade. Solar panels line the rooftops of the school buildings and provide bright lights in the classroom and clean drinking water for all the students.

But one thing hadn't changed – Sammy still dreamt of becoming a famous football player, just like Manno Sanon. And after today's winning goal, he was more certain of that dream than ever. Sammy looked at the big, brown dog who was wagging his tail so hard his whole body wiggled.

"Come on, Manno. Let's go home." Sammy switched on the solar torch he always carried in his backpack these days. "Mama will have our favourite snack ready. She knows by now that dogs and football stars love fried yams."

A note from the author

Nearly three million people were affected by the earthquake that struck the island of Haiti in 2010, and more than 200,000 people died. Thousands of people were left homeless.

My inspiration for Sammy was a seven-year-old Haitian boy named Kiki. He had been doing his homework when the earthquake struck. He ducked under the table, which saved his life. It took seven days for him to be rescued.

Scientists suspect that animals are able to feel an electrical signal generated by the movement of underground rocks before an earthquake strikes. This was my inspiration for Manno, the puppy.

Solar energy played a large role in the rescue efforts and the rebuilding of Haiti after the earthquake. This renewable energy source is being used today to light schools and hospitals.

Note: Soccer is the national game in Haiti, but they call it football.